THE SCIENCE BEHIND
NATURAL
DISASTERS

FLOODS

THE SCIENCE BEHIND RAGING WATERS AND MUDSLIDES

Dr. Alvin Silverstein, Virginia Silverstein,
and Laura Silverstein Nunn

Enslow Publishers, Inc.
40 Industrial Road
Box 398
Berkeley Heights, NJ 07922
USA

http://www.enslow.com

Library of Congress Cataloging-in-Publication Data:

Silverstein, Alvin.
   Floods : the science behind raging waters and mudslides / Alvin and
Virginia Silverstein and Laura Silverstein Nunn.
       p. cm. — (The science behind natural disasters)
   Includes bibliographical references and index.
   Summary: "Examines the science behind floods and mudslides, including
what causes them, their devastating effects, and how to stay safe during a
flood"—Provided by publisher.
   ISBN-13: 978-0-7660-2974-3
   ISBN-10: 0-7660-2974-3
   1. Floods—Juvenile literature. 2. Landslides—Juvenile literature.
I. Silverstein, Virginia B. II. Nunn, Laura Silverstein. III. Title.
   GB1399.S54 2010
   551.48'9—dc22
                         2008048026

Printed in the United States of America

10 9 8 7 6 5 4 3 2 1

♻ Enslow Publishers, Inc., is committed to printing our books on recycled
paper. The paper in every book contains 10% to 30% post-consumer waste
(PCW). The cover board on the outside of each book contains 100% PCW.
Our goal is to do our part to help young people and the environment too!

To Our Readers:
We have done our best to make sure all Internet Addresses in this book were
active and appropriate when we went to press. However, the author and the
publisher have no control over and assume no liability for the material avail-
able on those Internet sites or on other Web sites they may link to. Any com-
ments or suggestions can be sent by e-mail to comments@enslow.com or to
the address on the back cover.

Illustration Credits: Allen Frederickson/ Reuters/ Landov, p. 1; AP/Wide
World Photos, pp. 13, 16, 22, 26, 28, 32, 38, 40; Dave Gatley/ FEMA News
Photo, p. 20; Jocelyn Augustino/ FEMA News Photo, p. 42; John Shea/
FEMA News Photo, pp. 6, 8; Kaj R. Svenson/ Photo Researchers, Inc., p. 14;
Liz Roll/ FEMA News Photo, pp. 24, 35; Mary Marin/ iStock Photo, p. 10;
NOAA's National Weather Service (NWS) Collection, p. 30; U. S. Geological
Survey, p. 4.

Cover Illustration: AP/Wide World Photos

CONTENTS

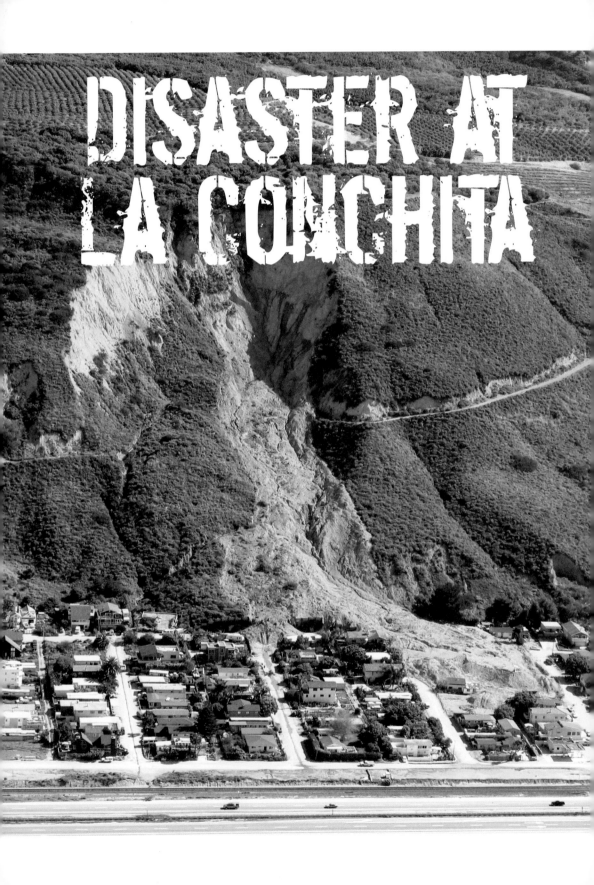

DISASTER AT LA CONCHITA

La Conchita, California,

is a quiet little beach community, nestled in Ventura County, northwest of Los Angeles. It once had a breathtaking view of the Pacific Ocean on one side and a pretty hillside on the other. But on January 10, 2005, a disaster struck, changing the landscape of La Conchita and the lives of the people who lived there.

After a series of heavy rainstorms in Southern California, a chunk of that pretty, green hillside above the town of La Conchita broke loose. A huge mass of soil and rocks went rumbling downhill. It rolled over highways and houses, burying everything in its path. Soon news media all over the country were reporting details of La Conchita's big "mudslide."

An aerial photo of the landslide damage to La Conchita, which occurred as a result of flooding rainfall in January 2005.

What's the Difference Between a Mudslide and a Landslide?

The big difference between a mudslide and a landslide is the amount of water involved. Both involve dirt, rocks, tree branches, and other debris moving down a mountain or hillside. *Landslides* may follow heavy rains, drought, earthquakes, or volcanic eruptions. *Mudslides* occur when rainwater or melted snow builds up rapidly in the ground. A mudslide is a mixture of debris and rainwater that can look like watery, wet concrete. This muddy mixture slides downhill in a fast-moving flow.

Mounds of dirt and badly damaged homes mark the landscape of La Conchita after the landslide that took place in January 2005.

Although news stories called the La Conchita disaster a mudslide, geologists (scientists who study the earth) later decided it had actually been a landslide. They found that much of the material that fell on the town was dry. Videos taken during the slide also showed dust in the air above the moving mass. Rainwater had flowed under a big chunk of soil and rocks on the hillside. That had loosened its connection to the ground and allowed it to slip downhill.

Just hours before the big landslide, smaller slides nearby had spilled onto Highway 101, blocking the only route between Santa Barbara and Ventura counties. Officials suggested that residents of La Conchita should evacuate their homes. But not everyone left.

As the landslide rumbled downhill, it ripped out trees and rocks and tore down power lines. Some residents who saw what was happening ran as fast as they could away from the landslide. Soon a thirty-foot (nine-meter) mound of mud and rocks had covered four square blocks of La Conchita. It destroyed thirteen houses and damaged twenty-three, as well as burying roads and cars.[1]

Hundreds of rescue workers arrived at the scene. They used listening devices and cameras to search for survivors in the mud and debris. Specially trained sniffer dogs helped in a thorough search of the entire area. Sniffer dogs help find survivors who

Ventura County Fire Department Urban Search and Rescue teams search and survey damaged homes in La Conchita.

might be unconscious or unable to call out loudly enough to be heard. The emergency workers dug with shovels and even with their hands.

The landslide disaster in La Conchita killed ten people, but there were a number of survivors.[2] Diane Hart, the last person who was dug out alive, had been buried underneath ten feet (three meters) of debris. In an interview, Hart said: "The house started collapsing on me and then it pushed me several yards with all the debris. I could feel the boards and the rocks and everything pushing me. I thought I was going to die buried alive."[3]

Authorities warned La Conchita residents that they could expect more landslides in the future. Some people have left La Conchita and moved to nearby towns.

But many chose to stay in their community.

What causes weather to

be sunny one day and rainy the next? All weather, whether it is calm or stormy, occurs in the air. Air is a mixture of gases that blankets Earth and makes up the lowest part of the planet's atmosphere. The weather is constantly changing because the atmosphere is constantly changing.

Something in the Air

The atmosphere contains moisture, mostly in the form of an invisible gas called water vapor. The water vapor in the air mainly comes from the surface of oceans and lakes as part of a process called the water cycle. The sun heats up the oceans, causing large amounts of water to evaporate, or change from a liquid to a gas. As the warm, moist air rises into the atmosphere, it cools. Eventually the water may cool down enough to condense, turning into tiny water droplets and sometimes freezing as ice crystals. These tiny droplets make up clouds, mist, and fog.

No game for these kids—their baseball field is flooded!

How Big Are Raindrops?

Raindrops are much smaller than you think. They may range from about 0.02 inch (0.5 millimeter) to 0.16 inch (4 millimeters) in diameter.

The water droplets in a cloud are constantly moving. When they bump into each other, they may join to form a larger droplet. When the water droplets or ice crystals become too heavy to stay up in the air, they fall. By the time they reach Earth's surface, the droplets have joined with many others and have grown much larger. Thus, the clouds return water back to Earth's surface as precipitation (rain, snow, hail, or sleet). This is the final step before the water cycle starts over again.

Air on the Move

Air is made up of gas molecules, particles far too small to see without a very good microscope. In cold air, the molecules move very slowly and squeeze together in a small space. They become heavy and fall toward the ground. When the ground soaks up heat from the sun's rays, the cold air above the ground also warms up. As the gas molecules get heated, they start to move very fast. The moving molecules bang into each other, forcing them to spread out and rise higher in the atmosphere. Thus, warm air rises and cool air falls.

Warm air and cool air tend to move together in batches, called air masses. These air masses move around the planet. So

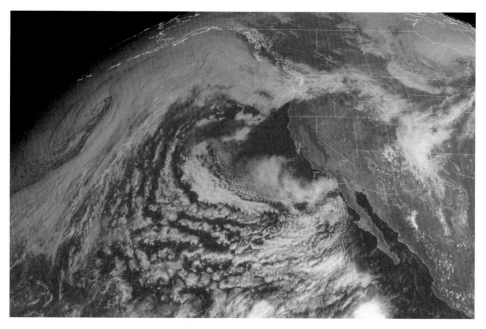

This satellite image shows high pressure over the northwest. The clouds over the Southern Rockies and southwest indicate low pressure.

the atmosphere swirls and bubbles like water heating in a pot on the stove. The moving air helps to spread the heat of the sun to parts of the world that are not heated as directly. But two air masses may come together and create stormy weather.

Under Pressure

Air is constantly pressing down on you with tremendous force. This pushing force is called air pressure. Air pressure is the result of billions of air molecules banging into each other as they zoom back and forth.

Air pressure is highest at sea level because the atmosphere there contains the most air molecules. If you climb a mountain,

Thunderclouds are large clouds that carry rain or hail. In warm, moist air, they can pile up into huge, puffy mounds that rise high into the sky.

the air pressure decreases because the air becomes thinner as air molecules spread out to higher levels.

You may have heard weather forecasters talk about "high-pressure systems" or "low-pressure systems." In high-pressure systems, cool air high up in the atmosphere sinks down toward Earth's surface. Air becomes drier as it falls, so the weather usually becomes stable and fair.

Rainstorms are low-pressure systems. They are more unstable. Warm air currents rise up into the sky in a swirling motion, forming clouds along the way. Air flows from high-pressure areas to low-pressure areas. When the two different types of pressure systems collide, thunderstorms or other storm systems may occur.

Thunderstorms

Thunderstorms are the most common type of weather storm. Worldwide, they occur as many as 16 million times each year. In the United States, an estimated 100,000 thunderstorms develop each year.[1]

In North America, most thunderstorms occur in the spring and summer. Tall, puffy clouds are clues that a thunderstorm is coming. Thunderclouds need more moisture and heat to form than other clouds, which is why they usually develop during warm weather. During hot, humid weather, thunderclouds may reach a height of more than 11 miles (18 kilometers).

Storm clouds can produce heavy rain, which can drop a lot of water on the Earth's surface. Weather scientists measure the amount of rainfall by the depth the rainwater reaches after falling into an open container. A storm can drop more than 2 inches (5 centimeters) of rain in an hour. Some of the rain soaks into the soil or is carried away by rivers and streams. Serious flooding can occur when the land in an area cannot drain the excess water left by the storm.

Why Are Storm Clouds Dark and Gray?

On a bright, sunny day, clouds look white because the water droplets they contain reflect the sunlight. A thundercloud is dark and gray because it is packed with water droplets. The storm cloud is so thick and heavy with moisture that it blocks the sunlight.

UNDERSTANDING FLOODS

Earth is sometimes called

the "blue planet" because most of its surface—about 70 percent—is covered with water, mostly oceans. In some places, land areas rise above the water. These land areas are the continents and islands on which people live. Rivers and streams cut through these lands, carving out pathways as they flow toward the ocean.

Usually the oceans, lakes, rivers, and streams stay within certain boundaries. Barriers such as beaches, cliffs, and riverbanks usually keep the water from overflowing. But certain conditions, such as heavy rains, can make the water level rise. If the water cannot drain fast enough, it spills over onto dry land. This is called a flood.

This aerial photograph shows the extensive flooding from the Mississippi River on April 16, 2008, near Vicksburg, Mississippi.

Can Floods Happen in the Dry Desert?

Yes. Although deserts are dry *most* of the time, it does rain sometimes. And when it rains, it pours! Some desert plants use these heavy rainfalls to grow and produce colorful flowers.

Soaking It Up

When rain falls to the ground, where does it go? Does it just sit there, forming a pool of water? That depends on how well the land can absorb (soak up) water. Some land surfaces absorb rainwater better than others. For example, soil can be very absorbent. It acts like a sponge and does a good job soaking up water. The water flows into tiny cracks and hollows in and around the solid soil particles. Most rocks, however, are not absorbent. In fact, water can flow right over their hard surfaces. The same is true for concrete and asphalt, common man-made surfaces found in cities and other developed areas.

Soil can hold only a certain amount of water. When the ground has soaked up as much water as it can possibly hold, it is said to be saturated. Once the land is saturated, any more rain that falls builds up on the surface and starts to flow downhill. This excess water is called runoff. The runoff flows along until it eventually spills into a creek, stream, river, lake, or ocean. You may have noticed how high a river looks after a heavy rainfall.

Going with the Flow

Rivers, streams, and creeks are part of a natural drainage system. They normally drain any extra water from the land. The flowing water gradually cuts channels (pathways) into the soil and rock. The water carries off bits of soil and minerals, and the channels gradually get deeper and wider. The ground looks like it has been eaten away. This process is called erosion. The solid material carried by the water settles farther downstream, when the flow slows down.

A "Greener" Park

When Cincinnati, Ohio, built a system of pathways in its Bettman Nature Preserve in 2007, city planners decided to use a new kind of concrete. They needed a hard surface that people in wheelchairs could use. But they didn't want to increase flooding. Pervious concrete was the answer. This material is hard, yet absorbent. It contains many holes and interconnecting channels. When it rains, pervious concrete catches and holds water, then allows it to drain easily into the soil below. Many communities are now using pervious materials for sidewalks and pathways.

If you pour water into a bowl, the water level can vary depending on how much water you put in. If you pour in more water than the bowl can hold, the extra water will spill over the edges. In a similar way, rain may fill or overfill the "bowl" of a pond or lake and the channel of a stream or river.

Congresswoman Eva M. Clayton points out the high-water mark of flood damage at a church in Tarboro, North Carolina, in November 1999. (The dark spots are molds that grow while the wall was damp.)

The water level of a pond, lake, stream, or river often depends on the amount of precipitation in the area. If it hasn't rained in a while, water levels will probably be low. This is because water evaporates from the surface into the air, and there is no rain to

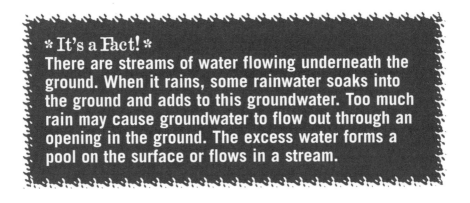

* It's a Fact! *
There are streams of water flowing underneath the ground. When it rains, some rainwater soaks into the ground and adds to this groundwater. Too much rain may cause groundwater to flow out through an opening in the ground. The excess water forms a pool on the surface or flows in a stream.

replace it. But a heavy rainfall, especially within a short period of time, can quickly raise a river's water level. The water cannot drain fast enough and may start spilling over the sides of the riverbed and onto

the floodplain. As the water continues to spread over the land, it builds up until the area is flooded—covered with water.

The Nature of Floods

Most floods develop slowly over time. After a week or so of heavy rains or melting snow, extra water causes the river to overflow onto the floodplain. These floods are fairly predictable—weather experts can usually tell when and where they will occur. Flood warnings give people enough time to get to a safer area on higher ground.

Some floods are fast rising. These are called flash floods. Flash floods are very sudden and come with little warning. They usually occur after a heavy rainfall, when rain falls too quickly to be absorbed by the land. Soon raging rivers overflow into the soaking wet ground. Flash floods are very dangerous because people usually don't know they're coming.

Floods can vary greatly in depth, from just a few inches (centimeters) up to 40 feet (12 meters) or more. After a flood reaches its crest level—that is, the flood's high point as it passes a certain area—the water level recedes (goes back down). The water may run back into the stream or lake, seep into the ground, or evaporate.

When Mud Flows

When rainwater saturates the ground, the soil gets very heavy and turns into mud.

An aerial photo of damaged roads and vegetation as a result of landlides and mudflows in Chuxiong Yi Autonomous Prefecture of southwest China's Yunnan Province in November 2008.

If this happens on a mountain or a hillside, the wet, heavy mixture of soil and rocks may break away and slide downhill. Mudslides can even occur after the rains have stopped. They can also be triggered by melting snow.

Mudslides usually occur during periods of heavy rainfall or snowmelt. They may start as small landslides that turn wet and muddy as they move down the slope. On the way down, a mudslide moves about 10 miles per hour (16 kilometers per hour), but it can quickly pick up speed, reaching up to 35 miles per hour (56 kilometers per hour).

What Makes Mud Flow Downhill?

Mud flows downhill because of gravity. Gravity is a force that pulls objects together. When you drop a stone, for example, it falls to the ground. It is the pull of Earth's gravity that makes the stone fall when you let it go. In a mudslide, thick mud has loosened from the hillside, and gravity pulls the heavy mud downward. It will continue flowing downhill until it reaches the bottom.

Mudslides continue flowing downhill, sometimes carving out channels along the way. The flow of mud gets bigger and bigger as it picks up more water, soil, trees, boulders, and other materials. By the time the flow has reached flatter ground, the debris may spread over a wide area. Sometimes a mudslide dumps huge mounds of mud that can cause serious damage to developed areas.

WHAT CAUSES FLOODS?

In August 2005 Hurricane Katrina,

one of the worst hurricanes in U.S. history, hit New Orleans, Louisiana. The storm brought powerful winds, with gusts up to 125 miles per hour (201 kilometers per hour).[1] The whipping winds pushed the water of lakes and rivers onto the shore. These rising waters, called storm surges, flooded coastal areas.

> *** It's a Fact! ***
> New Orleans lies in a bowl-shaped area from 6 to 20 feet (2 to 6 meters) *below* sea level. Levees (walls built from sand and dirt), topped by flood walls (structures made of steel and concrete), normally hold back the water. Pumping stations help keep water out as well. If any of these flood control systems fail, the city has a high risk of serious flooding.

Rescue teams search the flooded streets of New Orleans in the wake of Hurricane Katrina in September 2005.

In just a matter of hours, the floodwaters destroyed homes, roads, bridges, hospitals, and schools in Louisiana, Mississippi, and Alabama. The storm surge reached 10 feet (3 meters) high in some areas, and more than 27 feet (8 meters) high in others.[2] In New Orleans, after the levees failed, storm surges flooded about 80 percent of the city.[3]

Storm surges caused by hurricanes are just one of a wide variety of causes of flooding.

Stormy Weather

Many hurricanes have dumped 10 to 15 inches (25 to 38 centimeters) of rain in a twenty-four-hour period. Some storms

A man clings to debris in order to stay afloat in a flooded village in the Khurda District of western India in July 2001.

may bring even heavier rains, up to 40 inches (100 centimeters) or more. Such huge amounts of rainfall in a short amount of time can flood entire communities.

A storm doesn't have to be a big hurricane to cause serious flooding. Any rainstorm that brings heavy rains can cause flooding. A heavy storm can dump several inches of rain in a short period of time. If storms continue for days or weeks, there is no chance for the water to drain.

In certain regions, including South Asia, Mexico, and the state of Arizona, there is a rainy season, known as monsoon season. Moist air masses move in from the nearby ocean, bringing strong winds and heavy downpours. Every year, residents have to clean up the damage caused by monsoon season.

Rainy Season

The weather in "sunny California" isn't always sunny. In fact, southern California has two seasons—a dry season and a rainy season. During the rainy season (usually from late fall to early spring) it can rain for long periods, sometimes dumping three or more inches (close to eight centimeters) of rain in a single day. At the time of La Conchita's landslide, southern California had been having frequent heavy rainstorms for five weeks. Los Angeles had a record rainfall of 17 inches (43 centimeters) during that time.[4] During the rainy season, mudslides are common in southern California.

Melting Snow

Snow melts when the outside temperature is above freezing. Usually snow melts slowly, and the water just trickles away. But when the temperature rises sharply, or when heavy rains follow a snowfall, snow can melt very quickly. Soon streams of water are flowing from the melting snow. After awhile, the big meltdown can lead to flooding problems in some areas.

Melting snow and rain flood River Road in Moretown, Vermont, on Christmas Day 2003.

Tsunamis

Like storm surges, tsunamis can cause widespread flooding very quickly. A tsunami is a series of giant ocean waves. Tsunamis are most common in the Pacific Ocean. They have also occurred in other bodies of water, including the Caribbean and Mediterranean Seas, and the Indian and Atlantic Oceans. By the time they reach land, the waves have formed a huge wall of water—up to 100 feet (30 meters) or higher. As these giant waves come crashing onto shore, they can flood entire coastal communities and cause tremendous damage.

Tsunamis are usually caused by earthquakes on the ocean floor. But underwater volcanoes and landslides can also cause tsunamis. Landslides that occur on land and send debris tumbling into lakes or oceans can trigger tsunamis as well.

Drought

Would you believe that a drought—a long period of dry weather—can lead to flooding? When a region goes through a long period of little or no rainfall, the ground can get very dry. Dry soil may become hard and form cracks along the surface. Then it loses the ability to soak up water when it rains. You may notice something similar if you try to pour water on a very dry sponge. At first the sponge absorbs only part of the water. The rest rolls right off the surface, causing a minor "flood" in the sink.

Most regions of the world have droughts at one time or another. In the desert, though, droughts are common. When a long drought ends, heavy rains often fall in a short time, which can cause a flash flood.

When a Dam Breaks

Dams are walls used to block or slow the flow of water in rivers. They may be built upstream from towns and cities to reduce flooding. As water builds up behind a dam, it forms a pool or lake. Rainstorms or snowmelt may add more water—sometimes

This 1889 photo shows the aftermath of the famous Johnstown flood. Caused by a broken dam, the flood destroyed the town and killed more than 2,200 people.

enough to flow over the top of the dam. Meanwhile, all this water puts pressure on the dam. Workers can open floodgates in the dam to let out water. This helps to release the pressure.

Normally dams are strong and can handle a lot of pressure. But as a dam gets older, it may weaken and form cracks. Eventually, the water may force its way through the dam, causing it to collapse. If a dam breaks, the floodwaters could drown a whole community.

Some dams are not built, but form by accident. Fallen tree branches or debris from landslides can block rivers and streams. Then water builds up behind this natural dam. Flooding above the dam can happen as the water spreads out. If the dam breaks up, the built-up water will flow downstream and flood other areas.

Why Do Beavers Build Dams?

Beavers build dams in rivers and streams to *flood* the surrounding area. These water-dwelling animals make their dams out of whatever they can find, including grasses, brush, small trees, and mud. The pools that build up behind the dams allow beavers to get food and shelter without having to leave the water.

DANGERS OF FLOODS AND MUDSLIDES

On average, floods kill more than

100 people and cost $4.6 billion in damage each year in the United States.[1] Mudslides, on average, kill 25 to 50 people and cost $2 billion in damages each year.[2]

Water Power

If you turn on your kitchen faucet and put a hand under the running water, can you feel the water pressing on you? Now imagine walking through a flooded street. *Could* you walk through it? Probably not very easily, especially if the water is moving very quickly.

Are Floods Always Harmful?

No. In some parts of the world, floods help to enrich the soil. The floodwaters leave behind mud filled with minerals. These minerals help plants grow. Farmers plant their crops as soon as the flooding is over.

Flooding rains from Hurricane Mitch wrecked the tiny Mexican village of Tegucigalpa (left) in 1998.

Floodwaters are much more powerful than you can imagine. Flash floods are especially dangerous because they occur so suddenly. They can knock down power lines, roll huge boulders down a river, and carve channels through roads and hillsides. They can also destroy houses, buildings, and bridges. They can even carry cars through the streets. Floodwaters can also sweep away people and pets. Cars can be swept away in floods as little as 2 feet (0.6 meters) deep. People can be knocked off their feet in just 6 inches (15 centimeters) of moving water.[3]

Storm Surges

Storm surges wiped out much of the city of New Orleans during Hurricane Katrina. In a flood, the surging water smashes into buildings and washes out roads and levees. The storm surge may also wash away beaches and remove the soil around the foundations of houses. Even buildings that are built strong enough to withstand the winds of a hurricane may collapse if their foundations are weakened by the surging waters.

Flooding water blew out walls in this home. The house was damaged so badly that it was no longer livable. It was later torn down.

Floodwaters can also make people ill. They may carry and spread disease-causing germs. And after the floodwaters have receded, buildings and their contents are still soaked. Books and other items made of paper may be ruined. Molds and mildews grow on water-soaked walls and furniture and spoil paper and clothing. Their spores may cause attacks of allergies, asthma, and other serious lung conditions.

Mudslides and Landslides

Imagine shoveling two feet of mud out of your kitchen or living room. People faced with that dirty job are the lucky ones after a mudslide or landslide. Tons of mud or dirt and rocks sliding downhill can smash buildings or bury them completely. This can happen so quickly that people inside the buildings have no chance to escape. In 1998, for example, Hurricane Mitch killed more than 10,000 people in Central America due to mudslides caused by heavy rains.[4]

Erosion

Frequent flooding can change the shape of the land. Crashing waves and currents along the shore wash away the sand from beaches. This is a type of erosion. Parts of the coastline near Vancouver, Canada, have been seriously eroded by waves. Floods can also damage coastal marshes, which are important habitats for waterfowl, salmon, and other wildlife.

STAYING SAFE

Rain is a natural part

of our weather system. We can't stop it from pouring on our neighborhoods from time to time. Even though some places flood more often than others, floods can happen just about anywhere. Worldwide, floods threaten an estimated one billion people each year.[1]

Can Floods Be Predicted?

Weather forecasters need two kinds of information to predict a flood. They need to know how much rain is falling and also how much water the soil already holds.

Meteorologists (weather scientists) have high-tech tools that track weather systems day and night. For example, weather satellites orbiting Earth take pictures of the planet and its atmosphere and send them to weather stations on the ground. Weather radar

Eye in the Sky

NASA is developing a satellite system to help predict flash floods. The Tropical Rainfall Measuring Mission (TRMM) satellite picks up microwave radiation from the soil. The amount of this radiation varies depending on how moist the soil is. The satellite measurements can be used to map soil moisture levels over wide areas.

collects information on clouds and precipitation. Radar can also track where storms are moving.

Computer models have been developed to calculate how much water the soil of floodplains and areas around them contain. These models take into account not only the amount of rain that has fallen but also the nature of the land surface. The type of soil and rocks affects how much water the land can hold. The National

A meteorologist studies satellite images on computer screens at the National Hurricane Center in Miami, Florida, in August 2004.

Weather Service uses this information to issue warnings to people in danger of flooding. These warnings are sent out through radio, television, and the Internet.

Emergency Plan

In a serious flood, people can be stranded in their homes knee-deep in floodwaters. If that happened to you and your family, would you know what to do? It is a good idea to have an emergency plan *before* a flood disaster happens. Find out where emergency shelters are located, and the best and fastest ways to get there if you have to leave your home.

At home, keep a disaster supply kit handy. You'll need items to keep you safe in case the power goes out or your neighborhood is flooded. Pack enough emergency supplies to get you through at least three to seven days stuck in your home or a shelter, until regular services are working again. The kit should include:

- Flashlight and batteries
- Battery-operated radio
- First aid kit
- Emergency food and water
- Medicines and special items for babies, the elderly, and pets
- Protective clothing, such as rain gear
- Blankets

Is It a Flood Watch or a Flood Warning?

A flood watch means that flooding is possible for a particular area. A flood warning means that flooding is happening right now or will be soon.

Flood Control

Besides dams, another way to control flooding is a system of levees and floodwalls. Levees and floodwalls usually do a good job protecting low-lying areas from flooding. In the Katrina disaster, however, the levee system failed. The levees crumbled as the floodwaters came crashing over them.

Floodways also help to control floods. Engineers build them by widening rivers and streams at certain points. This allows the rivers and streams to hold more water without overflowing. The

This house in Grand Forks, North Dakota, is protected by a wall of sandbags from the flooding waters of the Red River in April 1997.

water can then flow rapidly downstream. People can also dig ditches to lead the floodwaters away from buildings so they can drain into an open area.

People in high-risk flood areas may use sandbags to protect their houses and buildings in case of a flood warning. The sandbags are stacked against the structure, overlapping one another. When the floodwaters wash over the sandbags, the sand inside soaks up the water and gets hard. The sandbags act like a sturdy wall keeping the floodwaters back.

There are also some natural methods of flood control. Wetlands, for example, are marshy, wet areas that can hold large amounts of water. They do a good job protecting against flooding on dry land.

Wooded areas help to control flooding, too. Land covered with trees, bushes, and other plant life does a better job absorbing water than fields planted with crops. This is because farmers clear the weeds away from the crop plants, leaving much of the soil bare.

Flooding Tips

Here are helpful hints for you and your family during a storm:

- Watch or listen for flood or mudslide warnings during heavy rainstorms.
- Do not walk, swim, or drive in floodwater.
- Move important items to the second floor or attic.

National Guard members respond to a flood warning in June 2008. They are stacking sandbags next to a levee in Winfield, Missouri, as extra protection in case the levee breaks.

- If local officials say your area must evacuate, leave right away and move to higher ground.
- Leave low-lying areas near mountains or hillsides.
- Stay away from power lines and electrical wires, especially if they are in water. Electricity can travel through water.
- Do not drink floodwater or play in it. It may contain germs that can make you sick.
- If possible, keep pets with you.

*   *   *

We may never be able to prevent floods completely. But there are a lot of things that people can do to lessen the amount of harm floods cause. Many communities now have laws against building on floodplains and other high-risk flood areas. Meanwhile, we can build stronger dams and levees and study other possible methods of flood control.

CHAPTER NOTES

CHAPTER 1   DISASTER AT LA CONCHITA

1. "La Conchita Mudslide," *The Official Web Site of the Community of La Conchita, CA*, <http://www.laconchita.net/mudslide.htm> (April 27, 2008).

2. Ibid.

3. Associated Press, "Hunt for Mudslide Survivors Ends," *CBS News*, January 13, 2005, <http://www.cbsnews.com/stories/2005/01/14/national/main666949.shtml> (April 2, 2008).

CHAPTER 2:   STORMY WEATHER

1. National Weather Service Portland Oregon, "Spotters In ACTION, Winter 2006–2007," *Pacific NW Spotter Newsletter*, April 2007, <http://www.wrh.noaa.gov/pqr/info/pdf/SpotterApr07.pdf> (April 2, 2008).

CHAPTER 4:   WHAT CAUSES FLOODS?

1. National Climatic Data Center, "Climate of 2005: Summary of Hurricane Katrina," December 29, 2005, <http://www.ncdc.noaa.gov/oa/climate/research/2005/katrina.html> (June 27, 2007).

2. Axel Graumann, Tamara Houston, et al., "Hurricane Katrina: A Climatological Perspective," *Technical Report 2005–01, NOAA's National Climatic Data Center*, October 2005, <http://www.ncdc.noaa.gov/oa/reports/tech-report-200501z.pdf> (April 8, 2008).

3. Richard D. Knabb, Jamie R. Rhome, and Daniel P. Brown, "Tropical Cyclone Report: Hurricane Katrina," *National Hurricane Center*, August 10, 2006, <http://www.nhc.noaa.gov/pdf/TCR-AL122005_Katrina.pdf> (July 11, 2007).

4. Lesly C. Hallman, "Mudslide Buries Small California Town," *American Red Cross*, January 11, 2005, <http://www.redcross.org/ article/0,1072,0_332_3943,00.html> (February 21, 2008).

CHAPTER 5: DANGERS OF FLOODS AND MUDSLIDES

1."NOAA's National Weather Service Announces Flood Safety Awareness Week: March 21–25, 2005," *NOAA Magazine*, March 18, 2005, <http://www.noaanews.noaa.gov/stories2005/s2407.htm> (April 21, 2008).

2. National Disaster Education Coalition, "Landslide and Debris Flow (Mudslide)," *American Red Cross*, 1999, <http://www.redcross.org/ services/disaster/0,1082,0_588_,00.html> (April 21, 2008).

3. NOAA, "Las Vegas Weather Forecast Office Launches Flash Flood Safety Campaign in June," *Turn Around Don't Drown*, March 16, 2007, <http://www.nws.noaa.gov/om/water/tadd/headlines-vegas.shtml> (April 22, 2008).

4. Frank Jack Daniel, "Up to 1000 May Be Buried Under Mudslides," *The New Zealand Herald*, October 9, 2005, <http://www.nzherald.co.nz/ location/story.cfm?l_id=36&objectid=10349358> (April 16, 2008).

CHAPTER 6: STAYING SAFE

1. "Extreme Earth: Water: Flooding," *Discovery Channel*, 2008, <http://www.discoverychannel.co.uk/earth/water/flooding/index.shtml> (April 2, 2008).

GLOSSARY

absorb—To soak up.

air masses—Portions of the atmosphere that move around Earth's surface.

air pressure—The pushing force exerted by the molecules of the atmosphere.

atmosphere—A mixture of gases, including nitrogen, oxygen, carbon dioxide, and water vapor, that surrounds Earth and is held by gravity.

bed—A hollow that forms the ground under a body of water.

channel—A long passage for water to flow through.

condense—Change from a gas, such as water vapor, into a liquid as the temperature is lowered.

debris—The leftover pieces from something that has been destroyed or broken up.

drought—A long period of dry weather; shortage of rainfall.

erosion—The wearing away of Earth's surface by the action of water or wind.

evacuate—To move out from a dangerous situation to a safe place.

evaporate—To change from a liquid to a gas as the temperature is raised.

flash flood—A sudden and often destructive rush of water down a narrow channel or sloping ground, usually caused by a heavy rainfall.

flood—The rising of a river, lake, or other body of water which overflows onto dry land.

flood crest—The high point of a flood as it passes a certain location.

floodwall—A structure made of steel and concrete designed to reduce flooding.

floodway—A channel made to allow floodwater to escape.

gravity—A force that pulls objects toward each other.

groundwater—Water that flows underground and is held in soil and rocks.

high-pressure system—A weather system in which air sinks down toward Earth's surface bringing calm, clear weather.

hurricane—A violent tropical storm with circular winds surrounding a low-pressure area of calm air, called the eye.

landslide—The falling or sliding of large amounts of soil and rocks downhill at tremendous speeds.

levee—A wall built from sand and dirt, designed to prevent flooding.

low-pressure system—A weather system in which rising, swirling warm air currents form clouds and bring unstable, stormy weather.

molecules—Microscopic particles that make up matter.

monsoon—A seasonal wind that brings heavy rains; a rainy season.

mudslide—An often destructive mass of mud moving down a hill or mountainside.

precipitation—Water that falls to Earth in liquid or solid form; rain, snow, sleet, or hail.

recede—To go back down.

riverbank—The sloping land at the edge of a river.

runoff—Rainfall that does not soak into the soil but flows along the surface.

saturated—Holding as much water as possible.

storm surge—A sudden rise in the water of oceans, lakes, or rivers that is pushed to shore by the strong winds swirling around a storm.

tsunami—An unusually large ocean wave produced by an earthquake or undersea volcanic eruption.

water cycle—The processes of evaporation, condensation, and precipitation that keep water circulating between Earth's surface and the atmosphere.

water vapor—Water in the gas state, formed by the evaporation of liquid water.

FURTHER READING AND INTERNET RESOURCES

BOOKS

Eagen, Rachel. *Flood and Monsoon Alert!* New York: Crabtree Publishing Company, 2005.

Gibson, Karen Bush. *Mudslide in La Conchita, California, 2005.* Hockessin, Del.: Mitchell Lane Publishers, 2006.

Prentzas, G. S. *Floods, Flash Floods, and Mudslides: A Practical Survival Guide.* New York: Rosen Publishing Group, 2006.

Shone, Rob. *Avalanches and Landslides (Graphic Natural Disasters).* New York: Rosen Publishing Group, 2007.

Tibballs, Geoff. *Tsunami: The Most Terrifying Disaster.* London: Carlton Books, 2005.

Woods, Michael, and Mary B. Woods. *Floods.* Minneapolis, Minn.: Lerner Publications Company, 2007.

Zakin, Susan, and Bill McKibben. *In Katrina's Wake: Portraits of Loss from an Unnatural Disaster.* New York: Princeton Architectural Press, 2006.

INTERNET RESOURCES

Michigan Technological University. "A Child's Look At Floodplains." <http://www.geo.mtu.edu/department/classes/ge404/jmparke/>

WeatherEye. "Flash Flood!" <http://weathereye.kgan.com/cadet/flood/>

National Weather Service. "Watch Out…Floods Ahead! Owlie Skywarn's Weather Book." <http://www.nws.noaa.gov/om/brochures/owlie-floods.pdf>

INDEX